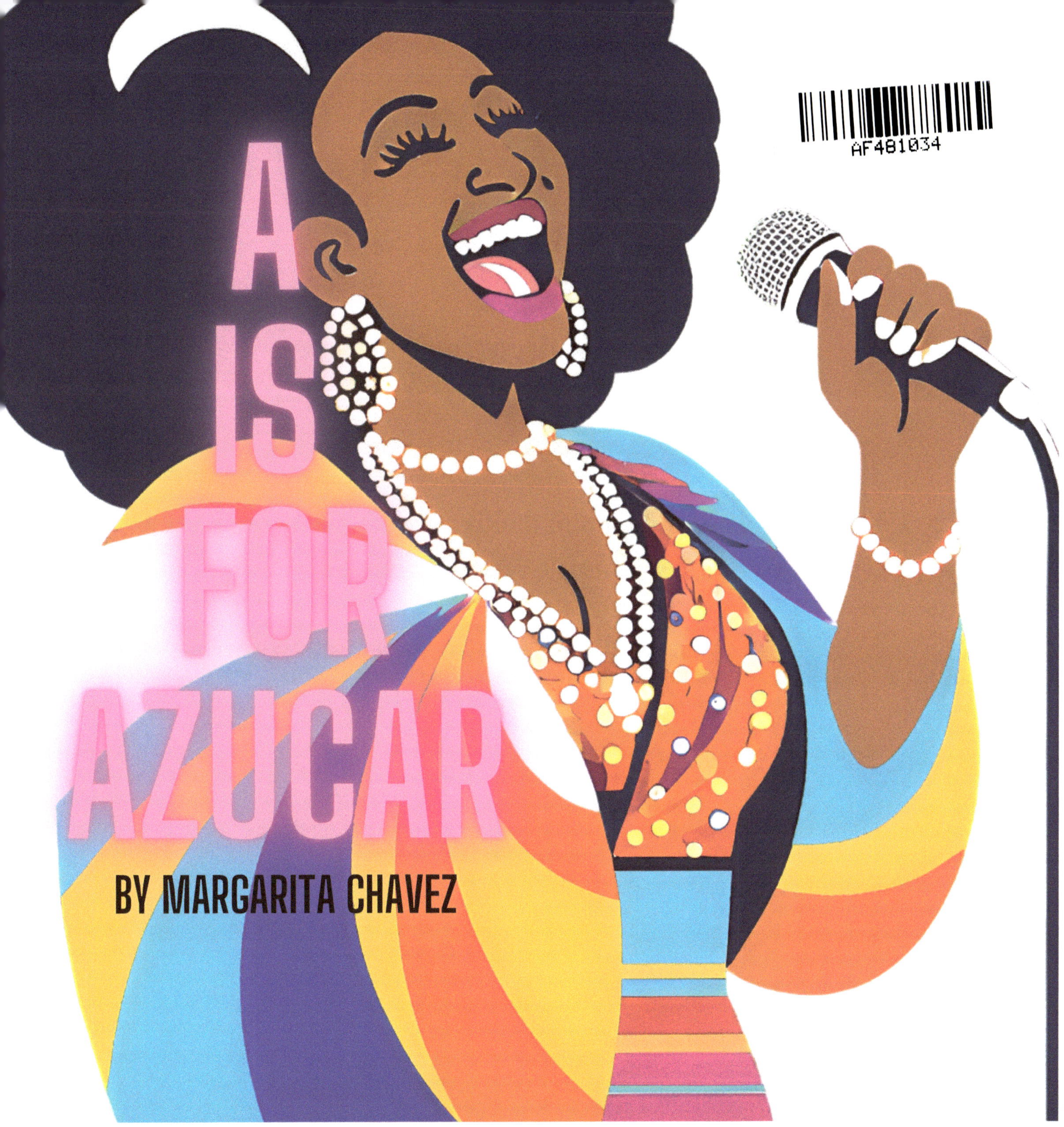
AF481034
A
IS
FOR
AZUCAR
BY MARGARITA CHAVEZ

Dedication

I dedicate this to my Cuban daddy, Carlos Ramirez Sanchez and my auntie Martha Sanchez.

Acknowledgments

Illustrations by Canva and Openart AI

A is for azucar, the Spanish word for sugar that the legendary Cuban diva Celia Cruz would belt out like a sweet anthem!

B is for Bolivia.

C is for congos, cars and Cuba.

D is for Dominican Republic.

E
is for
Ecuador.

F is for Filipino.

G is for
Guetemala.

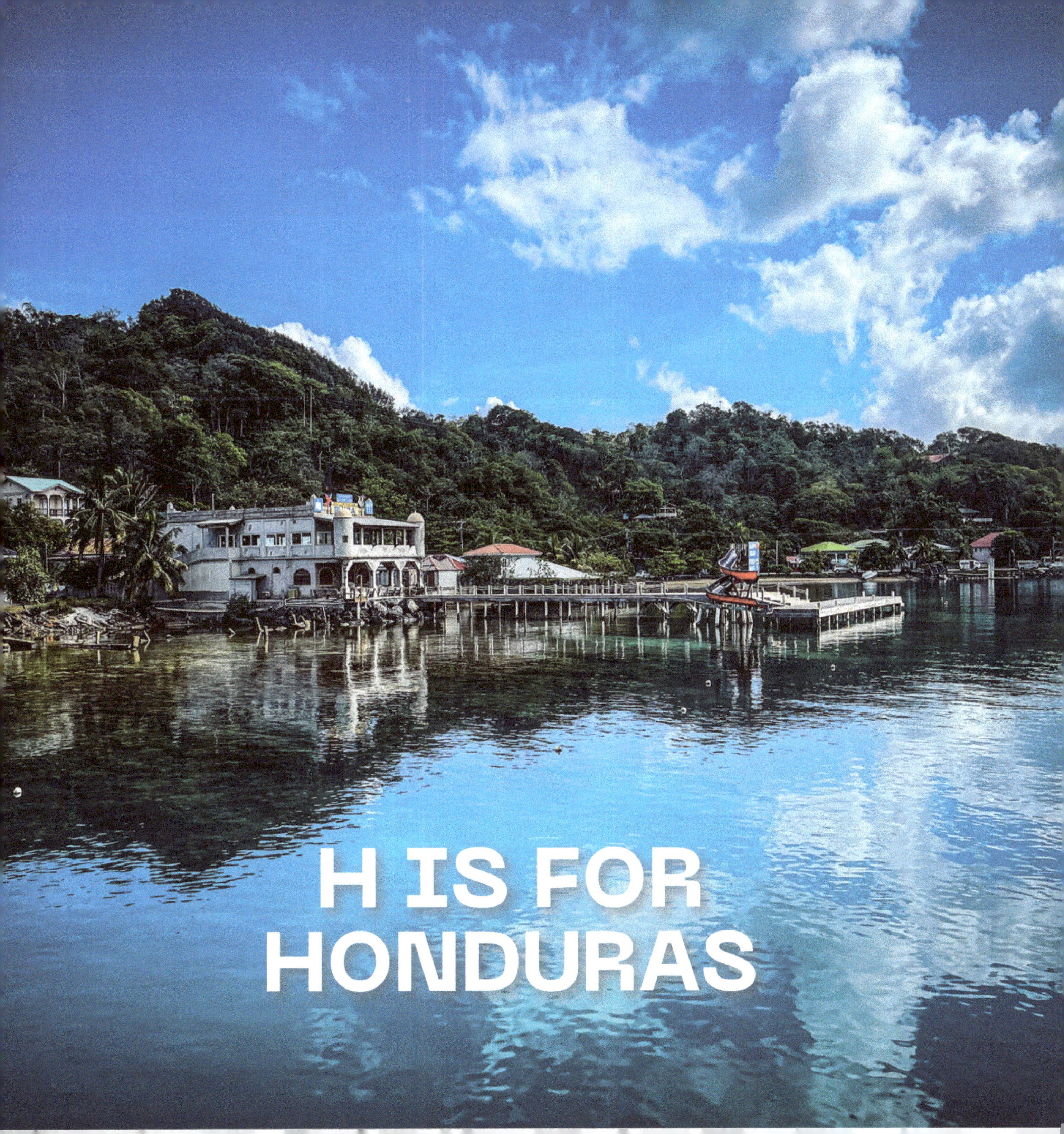

H IS FOR HONDURAS

I is for Iguassu Falls in Brazil.

J is for Joya de Ceren Archaeological Park, El Salvador

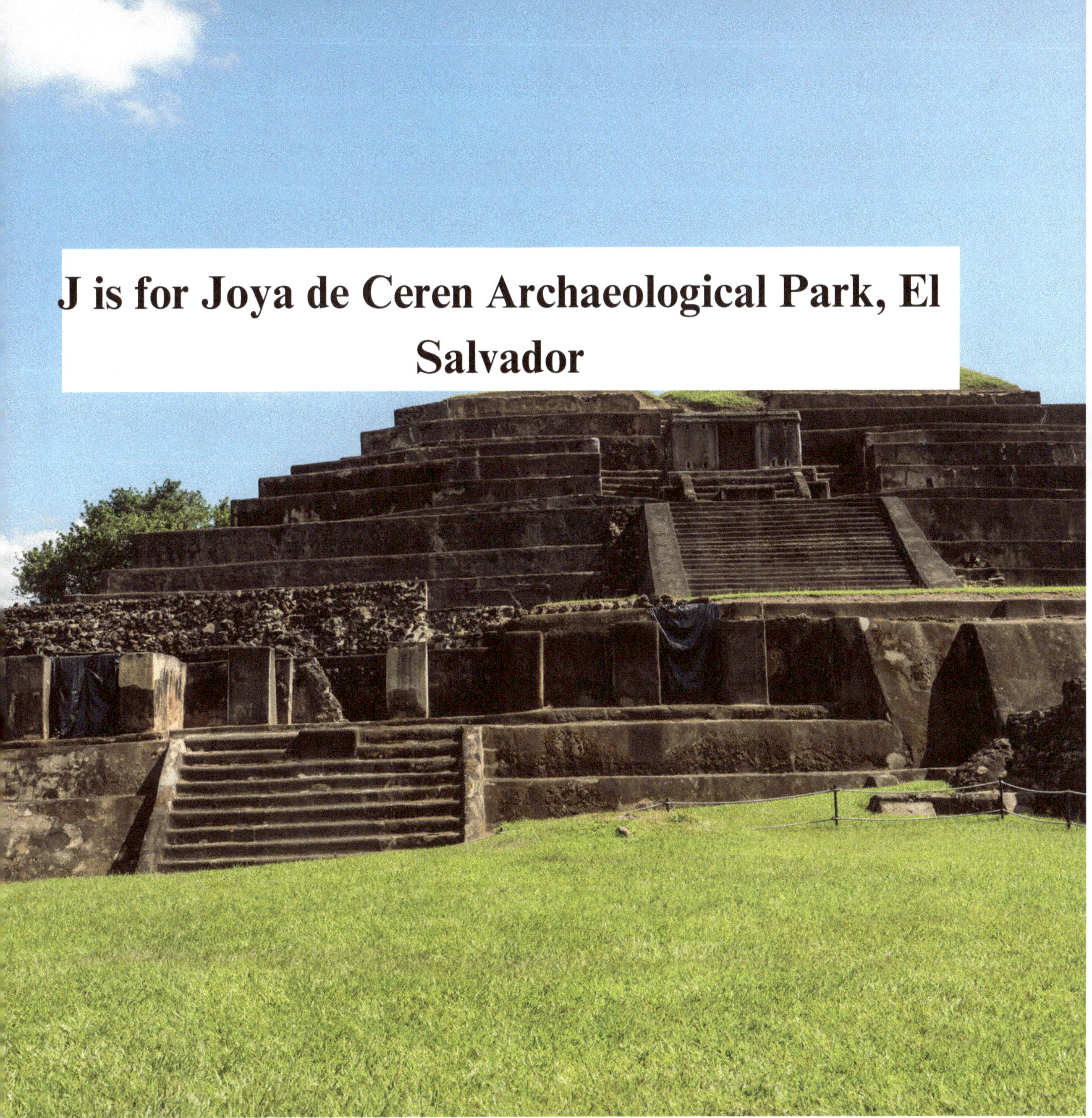

King Penguins, Chile

A decade ago, King Penguins re-established a colony at Tierra del Fuego, growing from 16 to over 100, with 15 chicks born in 2016. They are the second largest species after Emperor penguins.

Lima is the country capital of Peru.

M is for Mexico and mariachi.

N is for New Spain.

P is for Puerto Rico.

P – Panama Canal, Panama

O – Ometepe Island, Nicaragua

Q is for quinceañera.

R is for rice.

S is for Spain.

T is for Tortuguero National Park in Costa Rica.

Latin America is rich in culture and natural beauty, featuring over 100 UNESCO World Heritage Sites and Biosphere Reserves. Key highlights include Tikal (Guatemala), the Pantanal (Brazil), Torres del Paine (Chile), and Arequipa (Peru).

U is for Unesco.

Latin America, situated in the Ring of Fire, contains about 75% of the world's active volcanoes. This region is rich in volcanic heritage, with notable volcanoes such as Arenal in Costa Rica, Cotopaxi in Ecuador, and Pacaya in Guatemala.

W is for wine.

Argentina and Chile are famous wine regions. Mendoza accounts for two-thirds of Argentina's wine, and the Calchaqui Valleys have notable wineries. Chile's wine thrives between the Andes and the coast, with valleys like Maipo and Colchagua enjoying a Mediterranean climate. Cheers!

Xunantunich, known as the Maiden of the Rock, was a thriving Mayan city with around 10,000 residents during the Classic Period. Visitors can climb the 130-foot temple "El Castillo" for stunning views of San Ignacio, Benque Viejo Del Carmen, and the beautiful Guatemalan countryside.

Yasuni National Park in Ecuador is a biodiversity hotspot at the crossroads of the Andes, Amazon, and the equator. Its varied temperatures and high rainfall support millions of species, including insects, reptiles, frogs, and birds.

Zipaquira, Colombia, is known for its stunning Salt Cathedral, featuring a remarkable labyrinth of tunnels that present a modern interpretation of the Stations of the Cross, located 120 meters underground in an old salt mine.

www.ingramcontent.com/pod-product-compliance
Lightning Source LLC
Chambersburg PA
CBHW041838110726
48006CB00020B/2673

* 9 7 9 8 3 3 0 5 3 1 6 3 9 *